spot

BACKYARD ANIMALS

SALAMANDERS

by Mari Schuh

AMICUS | AMICUS INK

skin

spots

Look for these
words and pictures
as you read.

mouth

leg

What is that?
It's a salamander!

It is wet.

It is smooth and slimy.

skin

A salamander lives
near wet rocks and moss.
Its skin needs to stay wet.

spots

Look at its spots.
The spots warn predators
to stay away.
The skin has poison on it!

Look at its mouth.

It is wide.

Salamanders eat worms.

mouth

Look at its short leg.

It climbs.

It swims too!

leg

See the salamander blend in.
It is hard to find. It is safe.

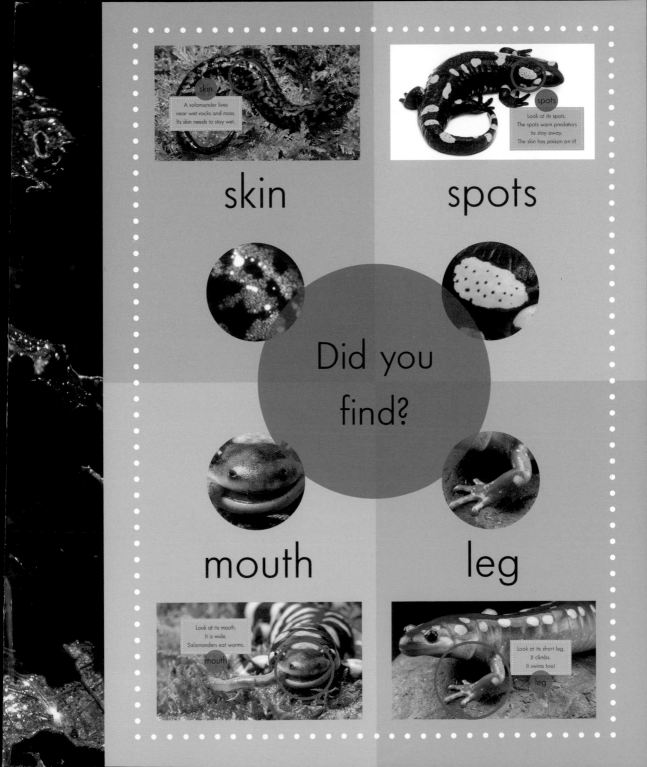

skin

spots

Did you find?

mouth

leg

spot

Spot is published by Amicus and Amicus Ink
P.O. Box 1329, Mankato, MN 56002
www.amicuspublishing.us

Library of Congress Cataloging-in-Publication Data
Names: Schuh, Mari C., 1975- author.
Title: Salamanders / by Mari Schuh.
Description: Mankato, MN : Amicus/Amicus Ink, [2019] |
  Series: Spot. Backyard animals | Audience: K to grade 3.
Identifiers: LCCN 2017053712 (print) | LCCN 2017054235
  (ebook) | ISBN 9781681515861 (pdf) | ISBN
  9781681515489 (library binding) | ISBN 9781681523866
  (pbk.)
Subjects: LCSH: Salamanders–Juvenile literature.
Classification: LCC QL668.C2 (ebook) | LCC QL668.C2 S38
  2019 (print) | DDC 597.8/5–dc23
LC record available at https://lccn.loc.gov/2017053712

Printed in China

HC 10 9 8 7 6 5 4 3 2 1
PB 10 9 8 7 6 5 4 3 2 1

Mary Ellen Klukow, editor
Deb Miner, series designer
Kazuko Collins, book designer
Holly Young, photo researcher

Photos by Alamy 10–11; Shutterstock
cover, 1, 3, 4–5, 6–7, 8–9, 12–13, 14

SALAMANDERS